PROCRASTIN

I asked my friends, "why do we need to stop procrastinating?" Their answers are here. This is a motivating list!

Never put off until tomorrow that which you can do today!
-Anthony Fabian

Because tomorrow is not guaranteed...
-Jimmie Tadlock

Because you don't want to let other people down, including yourself.
-Elizabeth McCormick

My mental health and my mental clarity depend on my ability to keep my task list under control. Staying on top of my responsibilities allows me to truly enjoy results rather than spend time worrying about whether or not they'll even happen!
-Darah Jewell

Putting things off is more painful than just doing them. Procrastination is a coping mechanism that causes more problems than it solves.
-Susan Masters

Because the saddest thing is a life of unrealized potential.
-Shawn Rhodes

Because I like heat, food and shelter.
-Stacy Pederson

Life is too short - don't regret what you didn't do!
-Ginger Watson Summerlin

Because it contributes to the buildup of stress.
-Jane Sidebottom Morrow

If delivering on your promises is important to you as a professional, then stop procrastinating.
-Jen DeVore Richter

You need to be able to trust yourself and what you say you will do above all else!
-Jodi Orgill Brown

STOP PROCRASTINATING TOMORROW

ATTACK WHAT'S HOLDING YOU BACK

Mary Kelly

© Copyright 2024. Mary Kelly.

All rights reserved. No portion of this book may be reproduced, distributed, or transmitted in any form by photocopying, recording electronically or mechanically, or by any information storage, without the prior written permission of the publisher.

Because the constant anxiety of not getting it done is worse than the stress of action.
-Tamara Ghandour

Procrastination means losing credibility, business, connections, trust, and integrity.
-Sheryl Roush

"This is the true joy in life, to be used for a purpose recognized by yourself as a mighty one, to be a force of nature instead of a feverish, selfish little clot of ailments and grievances complaining that the world will not devote itself to making you happy.
I am of the opinion that my life belongs to the whole community and that as long as I live it is my privilege to do for it whatever I can. I want to be thoroughly used up when I die, for the harder I work the more I live, I rejoice in life for its own sake. Life is no brief candle to me, it is a sort of splendid torch which I've got a hold of for a moment and I want to make it burn as brightly as possible before handing it on to future generations."
-George Bernard Shaw via Matthew Phillips

Life is just a bunch of memories – yours, mine, and others. When you die your memories will define who you are, so do it now.
-Robert Woodgate

Newton's First Law, that's why. Do you want to be the force or the object being acted upon? The person who doesn't want to do something finds an excuse; the person who does finds the way.
-Seth Hudgins

The length of time you procrastinate will be in direct relation to the amount of time it will take to actually get it done. Why wait?
-Nancy Hawley

They're called 'deadlines' not 'wheneverlines' for a reason.
-Brian Walter

You are stealing valuable opportunities from yourself by not taking action that you know will move you forward.
-Tim Marvel

Because having it done is better than having to do it.
-Maureen Burns Zappala

Because if I don't do it, nobody will.
- John Skipworth, Jr.

The world continues while you are procrastinating, resulting in lost opportunity and diminished results when you try to catch up.
-Tom Fields

Getting things done so I can reduce the stress caused by having things hanging over my head means I can increase opportunities for more business.
-Guyla Greenly

Procrastination on something is a sign that you don't want to do it or it's not in your zone of genius. It takes a lot of will power to push past that, so one must find a reason to do it that is bigger than the reason not to.
-Carolyn Strauss

I'd have to quote my buddy, Benjamin Franklin "You may delay, but time will not."
-Terry Brock

Stop procrastinating, and change your personal brand from being known as "Someday" to "Let's do this!"
-Suzanne Tulien

Because I'm getting older. There is less time. I may forget things. Tomorrow isn't promised.
-Steve Kelly

I don't want to be like Benjamin Button and progress backwards. I want to progress forward!
-Susan Ogilvie Bailey

Getting things done allows me to move on mentally and reduce stress.
-Lynn Ferrara Fagerstrom

It is never too late to be you and enjoy your life as it was meant to be. Procrastination is a choice. Choose wisely.
-George Tudder

Because it makes me feel bad when I don't live up to my potential because of procrastination.
-Mike Pennison

If you don't get it done, it keeps piling up!
-Mellanie True Hills

Because I need to live my DREAMS!
-Hollie Hart

Moving now helps me face my fears. If I'm procrastinating, I'm avoiding.
-Gregg Gregory

Procrastination means I am overthinking for a couple weeks…
-John Hand

Because it will only get harder/worse…because starting is harder than finishing….and because there is never a good day to do what you don't want to do, so there's no better day than today.
-Patrick Tierney

Because otherwise you become a procrastinator with no deadlines…argh!
-Lucy Lister

Life is fast and only gets faster as time goes by. I've learned not to squander my time by worrying, wringing my hands, and procrastinating. Carpe diem, y'all.
-Lesley Priest

When you procrastinate, you get new ideas. Ideas get a better opportunity to incubate in your head. You have more time to ask more people for opinions. Things change. You get information that didn't exist before. Sometimes it isn't bad.
-Yoram Solomon

Procrastination increases stress.
-Betsy Allen-Manning

Spend one day procrastinating everything you do every day...i.e., brushing your teeth, eating, exercising...you get the idea. How would you feel? Yes, not good at al. Likely, terrible! Now, think about how good you feel just thinking about those accomplishments, yet we don't. Imagine how great you'd feel and be accomplishing MORE! No more auto-pilot! Honor all we can be!!
-Lori Hetzer

The work doesn't go away or get easier. It just drives you even crazy as it hangs over your head for a longer period of time. Knock it out and then you can forget about it.
-Valerie Grubb

If not now when!
-Cindy Marty Korman

Life doesn't wait for you and tomorrow may not come! God gave you today, don't waste it!
-Kathleen Quinn Votaw

Procrastination is like having a bank account that continuously draws out daily interest… until you take the action to transfer it to savings.
-Richard Davidson

Life can end without warning. A decision or action delayed may never be made.
-David Hostetler

Because the list gets longer and the stress gets stronger!
-Dace Judy Ashcraft

Because it stalls forward progress!
-Barbi Hann

"For even when we were with you, we commanded you this: If anyone will not work, neither shall he eat."
- II Thessalonians 3:10 via Sheri Louise Schiffman

Unless you work in the history field where every tomorrow your work will still be history, then this book is for you!
-Greg Contaoi

FOREWORD

To all those seeking a helping hand and a dose of motivation to overcome procrastination.

Life often presents us with a barrage of tasks and responsibilities that can make us feel like throwing in the towel. It's natural to get sidetracked and find comfort in distractions when the going gets tough. But remember, you're not alone in this journey.

Sometimes, the challenges ahead might seem insurmountable, casting a shadow of doubt over your abilities. During those moments, it's crucial to realize that there is a way forward.

Breaking down colossal projects into smaller, manageable tasks can make all the difference. Each tiny step you take brings you closer to your goals, one step at a time.

When you catch yourself believing those sneaky excuses that seem to justify why you can't reach your full potential, it's time to take a stand. This book is here to guide you, support you, and offer practical strategies to conquer procrastination and unlock your true potential.

Let's embark on this journey together, and let the pursuit of your goals and dreams begin!

Let's get started.

"The really happy people are those who have broken the chains of procrastination, those who find satisfaction in doing the job at hand. They're full of eagerness, zest, and productivity. You can be, too."
– Norman Vincent Peale

TABLE OF CONTENTS

Procrastination Survey iii

Foreword xiii

Introduction..xix

Chapter 1 Everyone Procrastinates 1

Chapter 2 Can We Put Off Procrastination? 9

Chapter 3 When Saying *Yes* Creates Procrastination 13

Chapter 4 Where Procrastination Affects You 21

Chapter 5 Procrastination Excuses 29

Chapter 6 Is Procrastination Always Bad? No! 35

Chapter 7 Attack Procrastination 39

Chapter 8 The Science Of Procrastination............... 53

Chapter 9 Time To Stop Procrastinating.................. 59

Chapter 10 Attack What Is Holding You Back 77

Chapter 11 Quick Tips To Stop Procrastinating Now 95

Conclusion 104

About Mary Kelly 108

*"I'd like to stop procrastinating.
Maybe tomorrow…"*

INTRODUCTION

"The only difference between success and failure is the ability to take action."
– Alexander Graham Bell

Have you ever been frustrated with yourself because you cannot seem to get things done? Do you ever find yourself avoiding meaningful tasks that you need or want to do? Have you ever filled your time with unproductive activities, creating stress for yourself later?

This is ***procrastination.*** And we all do it.

This is not to be confused with laziness. Procrastination isn't willfully ignoring vital and important, or even enjoyable, activities.

Procrastination is avoiding doing what you need to do and filling your time elsewhere, until you are up against a wall. Faced with a hard deadline and consequences, you finally take action.

There are many reasons (excuses) why we procrastinate. Let's start with highlighting *why* and *how* people procrastinate to help you shift from a procrastination lifestyle to a proactive mindset.

Very quickly, here are a few benefits of this book and the integrated exercises.

Procrastination might just be one of those hidden habits you prefer to keep to yourself, but the truth is, more people procrastinate than you might realize.

How do we procrastinate?

- Undergraduates put off studying.
- Line staff workers put off projects.
- Sales people don't respond to voice messages.
- Physicians don't want to give a patient and their family bad news.
- People don't change their bed every week.

CHAPTER 1

EVERYONE PROCRASTINATES

*"Begin while others are procrastinating.
Work while others are wishing."*
– William Arthur Ward

Everyone has the tendency to procrastinate. The difference is that some people seem to overcome their procrastination inclinations, while others let procrastination negatively impact their lives.

Procrastination is typically a way to avoid tasks. It may be a reaction to being overwhelmed, often caused by overthinking.

Everyone procrastinates from time to time. How do some people overcome it, while others struggle so much?

Chronic procrastination can cause some serious problems, both personally and professionally. From missing out on opportunities because you are up against deadlines, to creating unnecessary conflict, procrastination can create significant stress. That's why beating procrastination and developing a proactive mindset can change daily outcomes and make tackling important tasks easier.

This interactive book is designed to get you thinking about:

- How much you procrastinate
- What triggers procrastination
- What behaviors to change
- How to become more proactive

Get the opportunity to dive deeper into the content on a personal level. From evaluating your personal habits to creating proactive plans to overcome procrastination, my hope is that you take away at least *ONE* tactic (hopefully lots more) to apply to your daily routine to decrease stress, increase productivity, and feel better about what you are able to accomplish.

While procrastination is universal, some people take it to the extreme. This can result in one of the worst feelings ever: *regret.* When people reach the end of their lives, it's the things they *didn't do* that cause the most regret. The opportunities people didn't take, the times they didn't act, and the things they ignored make them wish they had not procrastinated.

Overcoming procrastination can help you:

- Improve your overall success
- Avoid costly mistakes, fees, or penalties
- Increase your self-esteem
- Enhance your reputation
- Gain more free time to do what you value

Why Should We Pay Attention to Our Time?

Proactive people tend to be more successful. It's not rocket science that people who don't put things off tend to get more accomplished and be successful. It's not that they fear less or lack the desire to put off what they don't want to do; it's that they learned taking the right action at the right time feels better than living with the anxiety caused by avoiding the needed actions. The habits and activities that come with living a proactive lifestyle tends to build habits and discipline, which translates to a certain level of success.

Procrastination can cost you money. Have you ever opened a bill, set it aside, forgotten about it, and ended up paying a penalty because you forgot about it? The simple habit of paying closer attention to bills, due dates, and other commitments can save you money and other resources. It's one thing to be unable to pay your bills and incur a penalty. It's another issue when it is a lack of organization or overwhelm that costs you financially.

Proactive people have more confidence. Our subconscious is an amazing, powerful part of our brain. Our inner self knows when we are off track. Our subconscious helps guide us in making the right decisions. When we avoid important tasks, our subconscious keeps a running tab and repeatedly reminds us that we are not taking responsibility. This creates stress.

This stress can result in sleeplessness, generalized anxiety, guilt, and shame. Proactive people have confidence that they are doing the best they can, so they don't experience feelings of guilt or regret. Proactive activities give their subconscious brain a sense of security. Even though things may not be easy, proactive people tend to be more confident about their situations.

Procrastination can ruin your personal and professional reputation. I have a friend who is habitually late, and this habit is perceived by her friends (including me) as being rude and inconsiderate. She is not just late sometimes. She is *always* 20–30 minutes late to every lunch, event, or gathering. She does not realize that she is alienating the people around her. People have stopped inviting her because she now has a reputation for being disrespectful to her friends. I am convinced that is not her intent, but it is how she is perceived.

For many people, keeping to a schedule is not optional. Being on time is a sign of keeping a promise to yourself and to other people.

Procrastination can cause you to miss deadlines. While not everyone cares about dependability, most people do. Being able to count on others for one reason or another is valuable in a variety of relationships. No one wants to be let down by someone who fails to deliver on their promises.

Procrastination increases the chances you may fail to make a deadline, not value someone else's time, be unprepared, or take advantage of others. This can damage your reputation and label you as someone who is untrustworthy. Being proactive with your time helps you avoid letting people down, and enhances your reputation for being reliable.

Proactive people enjoy spontaneity. Have you ever come across an unexpected opportunity to do something fun, but you can't take advantage of it because you are already running behind? When you are not driven by procrastination and the scheduling crunches it creates, you have more free time for spontaneous fun. Taking care of your to-do list may be the difference between doing something unexpected and fun, and having to say no to meet a deadline.

While procrastination often feels like buying time, ultimately it probably costs you time and more. Knowing how to combat procrastination tendencies can help you unlock important habits that can change the way you procrastinate.

How to Best Use This Book

Don't procrastinate on going through this material! Give yourself time, and create a distraction-free environment to digest the information and spend some time working through the exercises. Schedule time on your calendar, pour your favorite drink, and grab something to write with so you are ready to make proactive changes.

Some people choose to copy the exercises so they can go back another time and reevaluate their progress. *Great* idea! Having a fresh copy can help you see if your answers have progressed over time. Awesome!

CHAPTER 2

CAN WE PUT OFF PROCRASTINATION?

"Procrastination is the bad habit of putting off until the day after tomorrow what should have been done the day before yesterday."
— Napoleon Hill

Procrastination is pretty common. About 20 percent of people are procrastinating at any given time.

Procrastination and laziness are not the same thing. Lazy people usually exert the least amount of energy possible for a task. Procrastinators tend to exert a ton of energy into their tasks, but they wait *and wait* to do it until the last minute.

What many procrastinators don't always realize is that procrastination requires far more effort than laziness or being proactive. Procrastination takes a greater emotional toll, and yet, it's very common. Lazy people don't have a problem avoiding things or putting in minimal effort. Proactive people don't worry about what needs to be done because they take action before there's a problem.

Procrastinators tend to worry and obsess over the things they know need to be done, but they somehow cannot seem to find whatever they need to make it happen until they are up against the wall.

The time spent worrying and being anxious about what needs to be done often causes:

- Sleeplessness
- Overeating or undereating
- Anxiety
- Analysis paralysis
- Shame
- Fear
- Physical symptoms (sick stomach, headaches)

Putting off actions that need attention causes a

lot of stress. Procrastinators aren't thoughtless people without regard for others. They are often highly aware of how their procrastination causes problems both for themselves and for those who depend on them.

Working Better Under Pressure Is a Myth

One of the justifications I hear from procrastinators is the misguided belief that they perform better under pressure. Usually, people who tend to procrastinate justify their tendencies by claiming that what they accomplish at the last minute is superior to the work they would have completed when they had more time. They claim that it is the urgency created by the time crunch that helps them become laser-focused. Some claim it is a lack of focus that causes them to only start projects at the last minute.

An argument could be made that their procrastination and surges of productivity indicate that they leave a lot of genius untapped. If their output and energy were not just limited to being crammed into short bursts of productivity, they would be capable of achieving far more.

Working better under pressure isn't so much about

becoming smarter or more capable in short time frames. Combatting procrastination is about exposing a lack of discipline and internal self-scheduling. The skills they think they display while under pressure are always there, but they aren't accessed until there is a short amount of time left on the clock. So, while you or those around you may claim to "work better" or "do their best work" under pressure, that's likely not the case.

CHAPTER 3

WHEN SAYING *YES* CREATES PROCRASTINATION

*"A year from now you may
wish you had started today."*
– Karen Lamb

We know one of the leading reasons people procrastinate is feeling as though they don't have enough time to meet their commitments. We also know having too much on our schedule can be an active or a passive form of procrastination. Essentially, we allow others to add to our schedule without setting boundaries, or we create busy work by cramming too many things onto our to-do list.

Being Helpful Is Important

Being agreeable is admirable. It's what helps win friends and influence people, as Dale Carnegie said in his popular 1930s book. Saying yes is often considered a characteristic of a positive mindset. Being willing to help others and saying yes to tasks can become second nature when you have a people-pleasing personality. As long as you have the time, energy, and stamina, saying yes can be a positive.

However, some people are so eager to say yes that they compromise their ability to fulfill their obligations.

What happens when you say *yes* too much?

Saying YES Can Lead to Overwhelm

When we say yes, it may be because:

We are excited and want to say *yes!*
We have FOMO and fear we'll miss out.
We feel obligated to be agreeable.

No matter why we say yes, if we say it too often, we get overwhelmed and we overextend our capacity. Then we get behind. Then we procrastinate, hoping to meet all of our expectations without sacrificing things like sleep or going to the gym.

At some point, you simply can't keep up with the commitments you've agreed to when you say *yes* to everything. The key is to analyze what's motivating you to say yes and ask yourself if saying yes will serve you in the long run. If we say yes to things we don't need to do, it can lead to poor time management.

What to Do?

Protect your time. There's only so much time in the day, week, month, etc. Protecting your spare time in addition to your available time is important. If you don't build in down time for things you enjoy, you may become overwhelmed, saying yes to things you feel obligated to do. Learn that it's okay to say you don't have the time to do the job with the attention it deserves.

Nice phrases to protect your time are:
"I will have the ability to start that project at the beginning of the third quarter."
"As long as you are okay with receiving that in a week, I can manage that."
"Someone else might be able to devote more time to this."
"I don't foresee having the bandwidth to handle this project."

"My schedule is 100 percent full right now."

"No. Thanks for asking me to be included. Now is not a good time for me to take on any more responsibilities."

It will help you protect your schedule, your options, and your mental health.

Prioritize your priorities. There is always going to be a wonderful cause or a wonderful person vying for your time and resources. When someone asks you for a favor or some help, they are often blissfully unaware of the many other people submitting their request for your time, too.

You've got to determine your priorities, or someone else will determine them for you. Determine what your priorities are. Say yes to the activities and people that are your top priorities.

Practice saying no. It's hard to say no when you are caught off guard or don't feel confident setting boundaries. Practice and rehearse what you want to say for various situations when you are to say no. Have routine answers to choose from so you are equipped with a proper and simple way to say, "No, thank you."

Saying yes can become a form of procrastination when you allow having too much to do to keep you from completing the tasks you need to accomplish on time. Become more proactive, and choose what you say yes to without becoming overwhelmed.

Flip the Switch from Opportunity to Distraction

One of the reasons people take on too much and fail to meet expectations is because they see everything as an opportunity. FOMO (fear of missing out) and being exuberant about a wide range of activities can lead to seeing everything as an option you don't want to pass up. It's important to flip the switch and recognize when an opportunity can be a distraction that's taking your attention and resources away from your priorities.

Flip the switch by analyzing how adding something new to your list of things to do might distract you from what you've already committed to. Learn to say no, or postpone an activity or commitment until it better suits your schedule.

Flip the Switch from Obligation to Priority

When you say yes to things out of obligation, it can lead to procrastination. Agreeing to things you may not want to do creates cognitive dissonance and may make you secretly resent the obligation. It's no wonder you put them off as long as possible.

Flip the switch by paying close attention to what your priorities are. Defining your priorities can help you set boundaries and refuse or ignore activities that don't align with them.

Shift Your Mindset

Flipping the procrastination habit to a more proactive lifestyle is all about shifting your mindset. Change how you view things through a different perspective. Recognize you are not obligated to say yes to everything. You are allowed to say no without being labeled a bad or noncooperative person.

Proactive people set limits. They recognize that in doing so, they are making their lives easier. There is less risk of letting other people down. Proactive people are less likely to feel overburdened and overwhelmed because they are able to manage what is expected of them. They have a healthy sense of their own self-importance, and they avoid feeling guilty when they say no.

CHAPTER 4

WHERE PROCRASTINATION AFFECTS YOU

*"Anything worth putting off is
worth abandoning altogether."
— Epictetus*

Procrastination Can Negatively Affect Your Health

Putting things off until the last moment comes with negative side effects. Our psyche knows when we are failing to take care of business. Procrastination can trigger physical and mental health problems that otherwise wouldn't be present.

Interestingly, people often seek counseling for a variety of topics including, but not limited to:

- Marital/relationship stress
- Anxiety
- Depression

- Work-related issues
- Substance abuse
- Disorders like ADHD

Once the layers are peeled back and the issues are dissected, procrastination can be either a symptom or a cause for these seemingly unrelated issues.

While the act of procrastinating may seem like a solitary behavior, it can trigger problems in physical and mental health that may be relieved by taking care of tasks sooner or on time.

Additionally, health issues can be compromised if we neglect our health, avoid routine medical checkups, or ignore healthy living strategies. Putting off medical appointments can lead to illnesses and diseases that are preventable when managed early.

Sidebar: Please schedule routine tests and checkups!

Procrastination Can Negatively Affect Your Relationships

Our personal and professional relationships can be negatively affected when we are unreliable. Counselors know that procrastination is a root cause of patient struggles and frustrations. The procrastination lifestyle bleeds into all aspects of life.

Procrastination behaviors aren't limited to personal actions like waiting until the last moment to pack for vacation. Procrastination can also impact work and interpersonal relationships. Since procrastination leads to missed deadlines and broken agreements, it can ruin trust, which leads to a lack of respect, anger, and resentment.

Many people who procrastinate manage a variety of thoughts and beliefs that drive their behavior. Some common underlying manifestations that people who procrastinate might share may be:

- Low self-esteem
- Fear of rejection or abandonment
- Harsh inner dialogue
- Difficulty coping with change

- Prone to frustration
- Rebellious against authority
- Poor concentration skills
- Prefer instant gratification

Low self-esteem can trigger procrastination. Being insecure can cause people to avoid risk or feel incompetent. This can impact their ability to make decisions, take action, or initiate action.

Fear of rejection can be paralyzing. If you've been rejected in the past, the fear of it happening again can cause you to freeze. It's no wonder you avoid uncomfortable tasks. If you're overly fearful of being judged or criticized, it can be intimidating.

How you talk to yourself impacts your risk aversion. Do you have a running dialogue in your head that comments on every move you make? If you tend to be too harsh on yourself, you're more likely to avoid important tasks.

Most people struggle with change. While change is a fact of life, most people struggle. If you resist change, you'll likely resist any and all activities associated with it. From big changes like moving or changing jobs to resisting policies and procedures, being inflexible is a leading contributor to procrastination.

Most people typically cycle through the four stages of change: denial, resistance, exploration, and commitment.

Denial:
"I am not going to learn this new software system."

Resistance:
"They cannot make me learn this new software system."

Exploration:
"This new system might be a better way for us to process our new project."

Commitment:
"The new software system has a few issues I am still learning, but it is better for the team."

Low tolerance for frustration can stop progress.

When people are easily frustrated, it can make them more resistant. Overwhelm and frustration are major contributors to avoiding an activity.

Being stubborn can derail tasks. Some people avoid tasks when they think the jobs are demeaning, hard, or boring. Being stubborn can trigger a false sense of superiority that tries to justify avoiding a task.

Poor concentration diverts attention. People who have a hard time with focus are easily distracted. They are pulled in too many directions. Their lack of discipline and focus makes it hard to see tasks through to completion.

Impatience promotes procrastination. People who need immediate gratification put tasks off that require more patience and commitment. They often lack the stamina to see things through to the end.

Once we admit we have a tendency to procrastinate, finding out why is the next step. These common traits can help us see how we may be lulled into procrastination. Once we identify the reasons why we procrastinate, we are better able to find proactive ways to approach tasks and stop putting them off.

Procrastination is an avoidance activity. It's a way

of focusing on something other than what's most important at the time. Additionally, procrastinators use a variety of rationale for their behaviors, which are also avoidant to taking responsibility.

Procrastination Can Affect Your Income

If you work for someone else, procrastination can create significant work problems. Procrastinating can threaten workplace productivity and cause your colleagues to feel anxious. Your supervisor and peers may be wondering if you will miss deadlines.

When you are late, it puts the burden on other people. Procrastination can increase others' workloads. When you are constantly late on projects, people doubt your ability to perform the assigned work. When people at work lose faith in your performance, it can lead to termination.

Working for yourself can make a bigger impact on productivity, since there may be fewer external factors pushing you to perform. That

can make it easier to put things off and directly affect your business and your reputation in the marketplace. But when you fail to deliver for your customers or clients, repeat business is not an option.

Either way, procrastination can affect your income and make it harder for you to get and keep work.

CHAPTER 5

PROCRASTINATION EXCUSES

"A perfect method for adding drama to life is to wait until the deadline looms large."
— Alyce P. Cornyn-Selby

When it comes to procrastinating, there are a handful of excuses people use to justify their avoidance behavior.

As a professor of over thirty years, I was always confronted by bleary-eyed students the day a paper was due. Many of them stayed up all night writing a research paper that had been assigned the first day of class. I heard all kinds of excuses for writing the paper at the last minute, such as **"I do my best writing the night before it is due,"**

and they coincide with other excuses gathered from other procrastinators, such as:

1. "There's never enough time to get things

done."
2. "I work better when I'm under pressure."
3. "I'm pulled in too many directions."
4. "I need time to process information and think things through."

Let's break these excuses down and see what drives them.

"There's never enough time to get things done." Procrastination is far easier when you decide that you don't have enough time in each day. This type of procrastinator has two problems: *failure to set boundaries* and/or *self-sabotage*.

Failure to set boundaries includes saying yes to things you know will keep you from your priority task, but failing to say no. This can be to intentionally avoid a task, or unintentionally, to create a time deficit in your schedule that justifies procrastination and make it seem like it's out of your hands.

Self-sabotage looks like adding items to your to-do list so you can't possibly get everything done, or failing to be disciplined during the day, resulting in doing activities that aren't vital but seem important enough to justify procrastinating on your main projects. In this case, *you* are creating the time deficit, not an external force. Playing video games the afternoon the day before a research paper is due is an example of self-sabotage.

"I work better when I'm under pressure." This is a myth that people use to justify procrastinating. They generate the false belief that they are more productive when they are up against the wall. The fact is, people work best when they *do the work.*

Once we apply ourselves to the job, without excuses and distractions, we are successful, and we complete the tasks well. It isn't about how close to a deadline we are; it's about actually starting and completing the work.

My dad used to ask me how I managed to do so much writing. "What is the secret? How do you get articles and books done?" There is no secret. The writing happens when I sit down and decide to do the writing.

As Mel Robbins reminds her audiences, you

cannot wait until you feel like it to get things done. You have to take the action.

"I'm pulled in too many directions." This is tied to shiny-object syndrome, chasing squirrels, or being easily distracted. It is also for people who are easily bored.

I understand. At any given moment, I am working on at least five workbooks, three business or leadership books, and I am always updating my Productive Leaders programs (www.ProductiveLeaders.com). We all have multiple competitors for our time. The challenge is scheduling the time and using it to accomplish what we want.

People who use phrases like "being overwhelmed" or "easily distracted" as justification for procrastination find it harder to stay focused and get things done because they allow multiple options to scatter their attention. Instead of taking ownership of their schedule and their time, they abdicate their scheduling power to their boss, their families, their friends, and various commitments.

"I need time to process information and think things through." This is another version of an attempt to justify delays. Procrastinators use analysis paralysis to avoid taking action. By overthinking and overanalyzing decisions, they never make any decisions.

If you have ever worked for someone who cannot seem to make a decision because they always want more information, this is maddening. We will never have perfect information. This form of perfectionism can derail everything from updating the kitchen to selecting the final design on a wine label. Spending too much time reviewing information, sorting data, or gathering opinions can prevent procrastinators from taking necessary and important actions, and often cause them to miss deadlines.

CHAPTER 6

IS PROCRASTINATION ALWAYS BAD? NO!

"You can't get much done in life if you only work on the days when you feel good."
– Jerry West

Is *ALL* procrastination negative?

Well, no.

Everyone procrastinates for some activities. Some things are best left to almost the last minute.

I live in an area where there are bears (and I love the bears). That means I cannot take the trash out until the morning the trash is picked up, because otherwise it tempts bears, and can ultimately hurt the bears, who are then attracted to residential neighborhoods. It makes sense to not take out the trash until right before the garbage collectors arrive. In some cases, not doing some things ahead of time is both helpful and necessary.

Sometimes procrastination helps identify your priorities. Procrastination can reveal truths that may not be so obvious if you'd taken action sooner. Procrastination can help identify what's really important to you. Since most people take action on the things they value the most, putting something off may reveal that you simply don't care about it as much as you thought.

If you habitually delay doing the tasks associated with your volunteer job, maybe you don't enjoy it as much as you thought you would. If you are late to a lunch with your friends, maybe you don't really enjoy spending time with them. Procrastination may help you manage your priorities and allow you to identify activities that simply don't matter to you.

Procrastination expands ideas. Sometimes people procrastinate when they don't know how to tackle something. It can take time to think things through. Waiting allows you to do research or creatively form ideas. Since procrastinators tend to be mindful of what they are putting off, chances are, your mind is working overtime thinking about the project or the issue at hand. When you finally do tackle the task, you may have more ideas than you would've had if you'd started sooner.

Procrastination can save you from regret. If you are too impulsive, you may have made some regrettable decisions. Taking action too soon has its own set of pitfalls. Though some people claim they operate by the analogy of jumping off the cliff and knitting the parachute on the way down, that can lead to a messy ending.

Procrastination could prevent you from making a poor decision or bad choices that have serious consequences. When our intuition and rationale are not in alignment, it may be a good time to wait before taking action.

I have a friend who is so quick to take action that she does not see the unintended consequences she creates by not thinking things through. She is smart and proactive, but she would be more successful professionally if she would wait until she had more information before making decisions.

Procrastination may help you accomplish more. If you are used to being busy with small things to avoid a bigger task, you are still getting things done.

If you fill your time tackling lesser tasks in an effort to be too busy to work on something else, you are still making progress.

I was a professor for over thirty years. I loved being in the classroom with my students and teaching, but grading tests and papers was a chore that I did not enjoy. My friends said that my house was never cleaner than when I had a pile of final exams to grade, because I used cleaning as a delaying tactic. Instead of grading, I did busy work, like vacuuming.

Who Are Active Procrastinators?

In some ways, procrastination is an art. Being able to manage your time in such a way that you get things done, even at the last minute, is admirable. People who stay busy while procrastinating are often called *active procrastinators.*

There's a fine line between normal procrastination and the sort that threatens your health, relationships, and even your employment. When procrastination encroaches on these three areas, it *is* a problem.

CHAPTER 7

ATTACK PROCRASTINATION

*"Amateurs sit and wait for inspiration.
The rest of us just get up and go to work."*
— Stephen King

Create a Proactive Mindset

This section gives you space and structure to contemplate the material and apply it to your unique circumstances. You may want to make copies of this section to keep a fresh template in case you want to rework these topics in the future. Many people find it fun and inspiring to review their progress and see how their life has evolved over time.

This section starts with an introduction to important ways procrastination can affect our work, health, relationships, and finances. Spend some time reflecting on your habits and ask yourself these questions.

Journal your answers or simply make bullet points; there's no wrong way to complete these sections.

Do what works best for you... *just don't* procrastinate doing it!

When I'm being honest with myself, I know I procrastinate in these main ways:
I clean things in the house when I should be working.
I waste time on social media instead of finishing work projects.
I make phone calls to friends.

1. _____

2. _____

3. _____

4. _____

5. _____

STOP PROCRASTINATING TOMORROW

While we may not procrastinate *all* the time, it is helpful to know the specific circumstances that encourage us to procrastinate. To identify the circumstances, it is helpful to finish sentences like these:

"I delay _____

when I am _____."

"I put off_____

when I am _____."

"I lost time this week because I_____

instead of _____."

We don't all procrastinate on everything, just some things. We can be proud of the areas where we do not procrastinate.

Areas of life where I *don't* procrastinate include:

1. _____

2. _____

3. _____

4. _____

5. _____

Areas of life where I *do* procrastinate include:

1. _____

2. _____

3. _____

4. _____

5. _____

If I had to guess why I tend to procrastinate, it would be because I…

_____

_____

_____

_____

_____

_____

_____

_____

Earlier, we listed some typical traits procrastinators share. Circle traits you believe could be standing in the way of you being more proactive.

Some people don't consider what drives their procrastination. You may be considering these motivators or root causes for the first time. Don't judge yourself if you suddenly realize that you may be suffering from poor concentration skills, or that you are easily frustrated. These are common, which should help you validate how you feel.

- Low self-esteem
- Fear of rejection or abandonment
- Harsh inner dialogue
- Difficulty with change
- Prone to frustration
- Rebellious against authority
- Poor concentration skills
- Prefer instant gratification

We also noted some very real symptoms created by procrastination. Were you surprised to learn that sleeplessness and eating challenges can be associated with procrastination? Based on the list of symptoms below, circle any that you experience that could be related to your particular procrastination. Don't worry about what to do about this yet. We'll take a deeper dive into the ***what to do about it*** aspect of procrastination in the next section.

- Sleeplessness
- Overeating or undereating
- Anxiety
- Analysis paralysis
- Shame
- Fear
- Physical symptoms

We also discussed four common procrastination excuses typical of chronic procrastinators. Did any of them sound familiar?

"There's never enough time to get things done." Procrastinators use this excuse to keep their schedules packed with activities so they simply don't have adequate time to focus.

How does this excuse factor into your procrastination style?

_____

_____

_____

_____

_____

_____

_____

_____

"I work better when I'm under pressure." This common myth helps people justify putting things off, with the false belief they are better when time is tight.

How often do you use this excuse?

_____

_____

_____

_____

_____

_____

_____

_____

Why do you believe you work best under pressure?

_____

_____

_____

_____

_____

_____

_____

"I'm pulled in too many directions." This excuse blames external factors like friends, family, work, and community for not having enough time or energy to get important tasks done. This is also tied to shiny object syndrome, where your attention is easily pulled from what's important.

How familiar does this excuse feel for you?
Not common | Sometimes common | Very common

How does this feeling of overwhelm impact your schedule?

_____

_____

_____

_____

_____

_____

_____

_____

"I need time to process information and think things through." Analysis paralysis can stop forward motion. While it's not always positive to act impulsively, it certainly doesn't make sense to overthink things and never take any action.

Do you find yourself with half-completed projects?
Always
More than I'd like
Sometimes
Never

Have you ever missed deadlines because you can't seem to make a decision?
Yes
Maybe
Never

What projects would you most like to complete?

_____

_____

_____

_____

_____

_____

_____

_____

Consider how procrastinating affects your health, your relationships, and your income. You can probably think of specific incidents when procrastination impacted you or someone you care about in a negative way.

As I reflect on my history with procrastination, I can see that I develop these health symptoms when I am procrastinating… (some examples could include upset stomach, anxiety, fear)

_____

_____

_____

_____

_____

When it comes to relationships, one way my procrastination negatively affects friends, family, and coworkers is...

My procrastination has impacted my employment (or self-employment) by...

_____

_____

_____

_____

_____

_____

_____

_____

Now that you've had some time to consider how you may be procrastinating, and what it means for you and the people you care about, let's start figuring out why you may be procrastinating, and what you can do to take the right actions to move forward.

CHAPTER 8

THE SCIENCE OF PROCRASTINATION

"Yesterday is a canceled check. Tomorrow is a promissory note. Today is the only cash you have, so spend it wisely."
— Kim Lyons

Is there actual science behind procrastination? Yes.

While everyone procrastinates, not everyone is a procrastinator. The difference is evident with someone who chronically procrastinates, despite experiencing the negative impact on themselves, their relationships, and more. Additionally, their procrastination creates shame and guilt that affects their self-esteem.

People procrastinate for a wide variety of reasons. Here are a few of the more common ones:

- Fear
- Overwhelm
- Stubbornness
- Low-level tolerance
- Anxiety
- Aversion
- Self-doubt

Ultimately, procrastination is poor time management. Poor time management can be the result of an emotional issue rather than a lack of discipline. Uncovering the trigger for procrastination can help. It doesn't make sense to learn tips and tricks for a proactive mindset and lifestyle if you don't consider what drives the deep-seated reasons for procrastination. Without unearthing the reasons why people procrastinate, it won't help them to give them new skills. Self- awareness is the key to long-term, lasting, positive change.

You Can't Fix What You Don't Know

When someone becomes aware that their procrastination is a problem, they aren't always aware that it's tied to an underlying thought or belief.

An example of how procrastination is manifested could be failing to submit an important application on time. The procrastinator may avoid completing and submitting the application because they don't know if they qualify for the job, they are afraid of rejection, they are worried about the interview process, or other reasons. As the deadline approaches, they feel short on time and finally just get the application completed quickly instead of thoroughly. The time crunch triggers justification for any shortcomings with the application.

Deep down, it's possible that the real reason they resisted completing the application could have been a belief or thought that triggered procrastination. Let's apply some possible reasons to this scenario:

- Fear
- Overwhelm
- Stubbornness
- Low-level tolerance
- Anxiety
- Aversion
- Self-doubt

Fear of rejection. Fear is a common trigger for procrastination, especially fear of rejection. Putting in effort only to have the effort, *or yourself*, rejected can be petrifying. Feelings of inadequacy can easily make you put things off. If you've suffered rejection in the past, it can amplify the procrastination habit.

Overwhelm with the process. Some things are just hard. Whether you've been unable to master a task, or are afraid of change or trying something new, it can be overwhelming. Wanting to avoid negative feelings is normal, but it doesn't make things any easier when you add a time crunch on top of doing something you're not good at doing. Worse, it can really make things tough when you suffer physically, socially, or financially because of procrastination.

Resentment for the work. Being stubborn or feeling like something is beneath you can trigger procrastination. Having issues with anger, superiority, or feeling entitled can lead to putting things off and stewing about it. If you feel like you *shouldn't have to* do something, it's easy to not do it out of spite.

Low tolerance for stress. Some people have a very low threshold for stress or being uncomfortable. At the first signs of discomfort, they stop taking action. They may put their head in the sand, or engage in other avoidance behaviors rather than take care of what's most important.

The activity causes anxiety. For whatever reason, some tasks trigger anxiety. Anxiety can be generalized, or it can be part of a larger mental health disorder. Feeling anxious about a task can easily make you want to avoid it and put things off as long as possible.

There's an aversion to the process. With this application example, there may be an aversion to some part of the application process. When we simply do not like to do something, it becomes polarizing. While some people just grit their teeth and do things they don't like, others put them off for as long as possible or simply ignore the task, despite the consequences.

Lack of confidence. When you don't feel qualified, worthy, or capable, it can be crippling. Whether it's low self-esteem or second-guessing every decision, self-doubt can easily derail productivity.

Getting to the root of why we procrastinate can help identify what limiting beliefs and barriers are preventing a proactive lifestyle. Coming to terms with what's really preventing action makes a big difference in how you approach, change, and stop chronic procrastination.

CHAPTER 9

TIME TO STOP PROCRASTINATING

"Procrastination is a way for us to be satisfied with second-rate results. We can always tell ourselves we'd have done a better job if only we'd had more time. If you're good at rationalizing, you can keep yourself feeling rather satisfied this way, but it's a cheap happy. You're whittling your expectations of yourself down lower and lower."
– Richard O'Connor

We've reviewed procrastination from a variety of angles.

We realize procrastination is triggered by inner thoughts and beliefs that make us want to put things off until the last minute or, at the very least, until we get a handle on our thoughts and feelings.

This can cause physical and mental disruption to

ourselves and our relationships.

If you ask most procrastinators, they will tell you they wish they didn't procrastinate. They admit that procrastination creates stress, worry, and consequences they'd rather not have.

In an ideal world, procrastinators claim they would kick the procrastination habit. They would master their time and energy to be more proactive.

While procrastination can create a reactive lifestyle, being action-oriented can help create the outcomes you want without the fallout caused by putting things off. Being proactive means ***creating or controlling a situation by causing something to happen, rather than responding to it after it has happened.*** Being proactive can help eliminate a lot of the anxiety caused by procrastination, not to mention the social, work, and interpersonal relationship problems.

> If you've struggled with procrastination, or love someone who does, you know firsthand the turmoil it causes and likely want a better way to live.

It's time to STOP procrastinating, and create a

proactive lifestyle.

Find Out What Works

If you've identified procrastination as a habit you struggle with, you likely know what doesn't work. Whether you busy yourself actively while you avoid what needs to be done or you simply put your head in the sand and refuse to acknowledge tasks, you have surely felt the unfortunate fallout that comes with procrastination. Finding out what does work is the key to busting the procrastination habit and becoming proactive.

Let's take another look at the common reasons why people procrastinate and start to explore what to do to overcome them and create a proactive mindset. Here's that list again:

- Fear
- Overwhelm
- Stubbornness
- Low-level tolerance
- Anxiety
- Aversion
- Self-doubt

Tackling Fear-Driven Procrastination

We've learned that fear is often a primary driver for procrastination. There are all sorts of fears that can cause someone to put things off. Generally, fear of failure is at the top of the list. Fearing that you don't have what it takes to complete a task or that you'll somehow fail along the way and be exposed as a fraud or failure is equally terrifying. Procrastination is oftentimes a satisfying alternative to taking risks and solidifying your perceived inabilities. Though you can avoid many of the feelings associated with fear of failure by avoiding a task, ultimately it must be done, or you'll suffer even more.

What to Do About It

Depending on the level of fear and internal conflict you feel, there are a variety of things you can do.

Attack the fear head on. Sometimes what you need to do to overcome fear is to jump in and be willing to fail. Learning by experience can be ideal. Most people aren't 100 percent successful at things until they do them repeatedly. Surprisingly, when people driven by fear take big leaps, they lessen the hold fear has on them. They discover fear is often artificial, and that failure doesn't always mean humiliation or worse. Sometimes the melodrama playing in your mind is far, far worse than any failure you might experience.

Get some help. If you feel like you lack a specific skill set to tackle something, get some help. Perhaps you're really smart when it comes to writing a report, but you don't have direct experience with the subject matter. Take time to find and interview someone who is educated about the thing you need to better understand. Watch YouTube videos, hire a tutor, or find some other way to get some help and improve your skill sets.

Admit the challenge and move on. Sometimes admitting you have a weakness is the best thing you can do. If you are fearful, it may help to simply declare it and take action anyway. It can help you to forewarn people that while you may not feel especially qualified for a task, you are up for a challenge, and that it could result in some mistakes.

In the end, facing fears, getting some help, and

admitting your reluctance are forms of being proactive.

Overturning Overwhelm-based Procrastination

There are many fear-based reasons people procrastinate, and there are also a lot of reasons why people feel overwhelmed with everything they need to do. Whether overwhelm is attached to time management, related to the enormity of a task, or stemming from confusion and anxiety about what to do, there are a lot of ways to become overwhelmed. Regardless of the trigger, the actions that break down overwhelm and eliminate it are universal.

What to Do About It

Determine where you feel overwhelmed. Does the entire task feel overwhelming or just a part of it? Hone in on what it is that's overwhelming you, so you can find a solution to deescalate the anxiety. If you aren't certain what's causing your overwhelm, spend some time journaling or asking yourself the question, *"What is it about this task that feels so overwhelming?"*

Break things down into manageable tasks. It

seems like an easy solution and it really is. How do you eat an elephant? One bite at a time. Take the big project and break it down into much smaller, manageable chunks. Choose one task that will naturally help tackle whatever overwhelming task is before you. If a project is large, be sure to give yourself enough time to realistically take action.

Schedule breaks. One of the biggest problems with procrastination is shrinking the window of time to complete a task. When a task is overwhelming, time is the biggest commodity. Knowing you are going to work on something that may require you to work hard, stretch your mind, or put your skills to the test takes energy. Building healthy breaks into your schedule can reduce overwhelm or burnout. Getting away from the task for a while to clear your mind or do something else can help build the stamina to keep at it.

Take better care of yourself. Overwhelm can be triggered by a lot of things, including the enormity of a task or the expectations of others depending on you. You can actually contribute to the illusion of overwhelm if you are not taking care of yourself. People who eat right, exercise, and pay close attention to their physical and mental health tend to be better equipped to tackle tougher tasks with more confidence. Eat right, sleep well, and maintain your health for an easier time being proactive.

Stop the Stubborn Streak of Procrastination

Attitude is an important aspect of procrastination. If you are afraid that you can't do something, admit it, and still do it. If you feel overwhelmed, but you can step into the uncertainty and try anyway, *you are on the right track.* But if you procrastinate because you think something isn't worthy of your time, or you feel superior to the situation, your bad attitude is the biggest problem. Being angry, stubborn, or entitled begins and ends internally, and must be changed.

What to Do About It

Get some anger management tools. If you routinely feel angry, are frequently at odds with other people, or have been told you have an attitude problem, you likely do. Anger management courses or counseling can help you identify why you feel angry and what triggers your anger. It's likely unresolved issues that are creeping into your current life and messing things up. The sooner you address them, the easier it will be to stop procrastinating.

Humble yourself. When staff at Disney are in their onboarding process, the group is asked to raise their hands if they are in maintenance. Generally, those hired specifically for maintenance positions dutifully raise their hands, while the rest of the group looks on. Once the maintenance staff identify themselves, the leaders of the training advise the new hires that at Disney, everyone is tasked with keeping the image of the theme parks pristine, which includes clearing trash or other tasks that maintain the cleanliness and environment Disney promotes.

Increasing Your Threshold

Some people have a ceiling, and when they hit their limit, they stop. This ceiling can represent fear, pain, frustration, and failure. Once people hit their threshold, they procrastinate. Having a low level of tolerance for fear, pain, frustration, and other negative feelings can result in giving up easily or feeling like a victim. Being proactive includes developing the maturity and mental stamina to do difficult things.

What to Do About It

Do something that scares you every day. Eleanor Roosevelt famously encouraged people to ***do one thing every day that scares you.*** Whether it's speaking in front of people or learning a new computer application, reducing the aversion to things that feel difficult or intimidating is an excellent way to become more proactive. If your answer to stress and being uncomfortable is to shut down, then you'll likely stay stuck in procrastination mode.

Embrace pain and discomfort. When athletes want to improve their abilities, they increase their tolerance for pain. Pushing their bodies to new heights requires them to lift more weights, push themselves harder, and endure more, both physically and mentally. Their willingness to endure and embrace pain as part of the natural process helps them achieve greater success.

It's the same for a proactive lifestyle. Knowing that there will be some degree of being uncomfortable and knowing you can make it through prepares you mentally for the current and future challenges. Rather than put things off because you think you can't stand the discomfort, embrace it, knowing that it makes you better and stronger.

Immerse yourself. My friend Marilyn Sherman is a Hall of Fame Motivational Speaker who recently enrolled in a three-week French immersion program in Paris. It was not convenient. It was not easy. It was very effective. She vastly improved her French language proficiency, increased her confidence, and expanded her vocabulary. It took studying, classwork, and a concerted effort to not revert to speaking English.

Immersion therapy helps people tackle their fears and anxieties because they are in a situation where is no other option. By being forced to only speak French, Marilyn had to rely on the French she knew, and learn new words and phrases. She increased her proficiency in ways that would otherwise take years or even decades.

While immersion therapy can also include exposure to scary things like snakes and spiders, it's a great way to make everyday challenges more viable. Focus on not having other options except to do what you need to do. Immerse yourself in the task.

Reduce Anxiety-induced Procrastination

Feeling anxious is a trigger for procrastination. When something gives you anxiety, it's natural to want to avoid it. The root cause for the anxiety may only be a small portion of the task you need to do. Breaking things down can help you reduce anxiety and accomplish whatever is necessary, whether it is taking a test, tackling an interview, or keeping track of your busy schedule.

What to Do About It

Keep the main thing the main thing. If you tend to suffer from anxiety-induced procrastination, you're likely overthinking or projecting too far ahead. Proactive people keep the most important tasks at hand on their radar and relegate other tasks until later.

Stop putting all the eggs into one giant basket. All-or-nothing thinking is a huge trigger for anxiety. Looking at a task in its entirety and telling yourself that your entire future depends on this one thing can cause you to freeze into inactivity.

Instead, take a proactive stance and break the task into smaller, more manageable pieces. Allow for the right amount of time for the individual tasks—not too much more, or you might be tempted to procrastinate. If you need to make fifty sales calls, it's easier to commit to making ten per day for five days than be overwhelmed with fifty calls at one time.

Learn to relax. If you tend to experience anxiety-induced procrastination, you likely experience anxiety in other areas of life as well. Learning to relax and reduce anxiety overall can help you avoid procrastination. Whether it's yoga, journaling, practicing daily gratitude, or meditating, relaxation techniques can improve your overall ability to be more proactive.

Removing Your Aversions

People tend to put off what they don't like or don't want to do. It makes sense. Why waste time doing things that we don't like doing? I tell people that this is why we call work, "Work." If it was fun all of the time, it would be a hobby.

Some things have to be done, whether we want to do them or not.

Putting off tasks only delays the activity and causes

us to worry, right up until we take care of business. Having an aversion to something doesn't mean you can't tackle it and get it over with.

Proactive people understand something Mark Twain wrote long ago—If the worst thing you do in the morning is eat a frog, then you can get through the rest of the day knowing the worst is behind you.

What to Do About It

Eat that frog! Mark Twain's wisdom is right. If you have something to do that you don't enjoy, get it done and off your plate as soon as possible. Tackle the most unpleasant tasks you have right away and get them behind you.

When I was a student, I used to do the homework I struggled with first, leaving the homework from the classes I enjoyed for later. I called it my Homework Dessert. Because the difficult classwork was finished, I was able to enjoy the rest of my homework. When you do this at work, you feel proud of the accomplishment, and you can move on to what you enjoy doing.

Just do it. Like Nike says, "Just Do It." Sometimes

there's no way around an unpleasant task. Someone's got to clean the barn, do the research, write the paper, and take out the trash. Developing a mindset of *"I can do this"* helps proactive people get things accomplished with minimal aversion.

Do the difficult things often. Sometimes we have an aversion to unpleasant things, so we avoid them. When we avoid doing difficult things, this becomes normalized.

Imagine a surgeon learning how to perform a life-saving operation. In the beginning, many aspects of surgery are new and uncomfortable. The more the surgeon practices, the more normalized the various aspects of surgery become. Ultimately, what once was an aversion loses its negative impact. If you avoid something because it's intimidating or tough, it may be best to tackle it so it becomes routine and normal.

Banish Self-doubt and Procrastination

"Don't stop yourself from greatness before you've begun from fear or from self-doubt. You were put here on this planet to do great things."
— Kaiden Blake

When we aren't sure of our worth, our value, or our ability to deliver, it can be very hard to be proactive. To people who experience self-doubt, it seems that only confident people are proactive.

Is that really true? No.

More important than confidence, taking action, even small steps in the right direction, is what is needed to stop procrastination. It's normal to doubt yourself from time to time, but chronic self-doubt can lead to procrastinating when you don't feel qualified or confident.

What to Do About It

Don't give in to imposter syndrome. Everyone has an area of their life where they don't feel 100 percent competent. A common fear for many people is imposter syndrome. This is the worry that we may be exposed as an imposter—for pretending to be someone or something we are not.

Realizing that no one is good at every single thing can help you relax. Give yourself credit when deserved, and be encouraged by progress. If you suffer from self-doubt, counseling, coaching, a support group, or developing advanced skills may help.

When in doubt, figure it out! Self-doubt is normal. Use self-doubt as an incentive to overcome procrastination. Allow yourself the opportunity to be less than perfect, miss a step, or even fail. As long as you use the experience to help you get better, you are making progress. Sometimes people have to try and sometimes fail to move forward. Over time, taking action in the right direction will morph doubt into confidence.

Develop discipline. Sometimes we need some tough talk. It's okay to admit when we are weak and need some focus. Developing a disciplined mindset and taking action—whether we want to or not—makes a difference.

One of the questions I ask people who say they lack discipline is, "What do you want? Are you willing to do what it takes?" Then schedule it and do it.

CHAPTER 10

ATTACK WHAT IS HOLDING YOU BACK

"Until you value yourself, you will not value your time. Until you value your time, you will not do anything with it." – M. Scott Peck

This section helps break down *why* we procrastinate and what we can do about it. It is helpful to break down the various reasons for procrastination and see how they impact daily activities.

Again, here are seven typical reasons why people procrastinate. **Circle** the ones you identify with most. Add in your own reasons as well.

- Fear
- Overwhelm
- Stubbornness
- Low-level tolerance for stress
- Anxiety

- Aversion
- Self-doubt

Find the corresponding reason(s) and dive deeper into how they are impacting your life and causing you to procrastinate. Remember, getting to the root issues of why you procrastinate is a great step in correcting the behavior. It is hard to make a positive change unless you know what's driving you.

Fear

If you circled *fear...*

Fear is a common trigger for procrastination, especially fear of rejection. Putting in effort only to have you or your efforts be rejected can be awful. Feelings of inadequacy can easily make you put things off. If you've suffered rejection in the past, it can amplify the procrastination habit.

How does fear trigger you to procrastinate?

_____

_____

_____

_____

_____

What did you learn after reading about the correlation between fear and procrastination that can help you tackle your fears and stop putting things off?

_____

_____

_____

_____

_____

What help do you think you need to really tackle your fear-based procrastination?

_____

_____

_____

_____

_____

My action plan to tackle fear is: (Make a list of the action steps you plan to take to become proactive)

_____

_____

_____

_____

_____

Overwhelm

If you circled *overwhelm*...

Some things are just hard. Whether you've been unable to master a task, or are afraid of change or trying something new, it can be overwhelming.

Wanting to avoiding the feelings that come up is normal, but it doesn't make things any easier when you add a time crunch on top of doing something you're not good at. Worse, it can make things tough when you suffer physically, socially, or financially because of procrastination.

How does overwhelm trigger you to procrastinate?

_____

_____

_____

_____

_____

What do you know now after reading about the correlation between overwhelm and procrastination that can help you manage your to-do list and the overabundance?

_____

_____

_____

_____

_____

What help do you think you need to really tackle your overwhelm-based procrastination?

_____

_____

_____

_____

My action plan to tackle overwhelm is: (Make a list of the action steps you plan to take to become proactive)

_____

_____

_____

_____

_____

Stubbornness

If you circled stubbornness...

Being stubborn or feeling like something is beneath you can trigger procrastination. Having issues with anger, superiority, or feeling entitled can lead to putting things off and stewing about it. If you feel like you *shouldn't* have to do something, it's easy to avoid doing it out of spite.

How does being stubborn trigger you to procrastinate?

_____

_____

_____

_____

_____

What do you know now after reading about the correlation between being stubborn and procrastination that can help you tackle your stubborn behavior and stop putting things off?

_____

_____

_____

_____

_____

What help do you think you need to really tackle your bad attitude-based procrastination?

_____

_____

_____

_____

_____

My action plan to tackle stubbornness is: (Make a list of the action steps you plan to take to become proactive)

_____

_____

_____

_____

_____

Low-level Tolerance for Stress

If you circled low-level tolerance for stress...

Some people have a very low threshold for stress or being uncomfortable. At the first sign of discomfort, they stop taking action. They often put their head in the sand, or engage in other behaviors rather than take care of what's most important.

How does a low tolerance for stress lead you to procrastinate?

_____

_____

_____

_____

_____

What do you know now after reading about the correlation between a low threshold for stress and procrastination that can help you increase?

_____

_____

_____

_____

_____

What help do you think you need to really tackle your stress-based procrastination?

_____

_____

_____

_____

_____

My plan to tackle stress-based procrastination is: (Make a list of the action steps you plan to take to become proactive)

_____

_____

_____

_____

_____

Anxiety

If you circled *anxiety*...

For whatever reason, some tasks trigger anxiety. Anxiety can be generalized or it can be part of a larger mental health disorder. Feeling anxious about a task can easily make you want to avoid it and put things off as long as possible.

How does anxiety lead you to procrastinate?

_____

_____

_____

_____

_____

What do you know now after reading about the correlation between anxiety and procrastination that can help you reduce your anxiousness and become proactive?

_____

_____

_____

_____

_____

What help do you think you need to really tackle your anxiety-based procrastination?

_____

_____

_____

_____

_____

My action plan to tackle anxiousness is: (Make a list of the action steps you plan to take to become proactive)

_____

_____

_____

_____

_____

Aversion

If you circled *aversion*...

In the example of applying for a job, there may be an aversion to some part of the application process. When we simply do *not* like to do something, it becomes polarizing. While some people just grit their teeth and do things they don't like, others put it off for as long as possible or simply ignore the task despite the consequences.

How does not liking a task make you procrastinate?

_____

_____

_____

_____

_____

What do you know now after reading about aversion that can help you tackle your resistance?

_____

_____

_____

_____

_____

What help do you think you need to really tackle your aversion-based procrastination?

_____

_____

_____

_____

_____

My plan to tackle aversion is: (Make a list of the action steps you plan to take to become proactive)

_____

_____

_____

_____

_____

Self-doubt

If you circled *self-doubt*...

When you don't feel qualified, worthy, or capable, the reservations can be crippling. Whether it's low self-esteem or second-guessing every decision, self-doubt can easily derail productivity.

How does self-doubt lead you to procrastinate?

_____

_____

_____

_____

_____

What help do you think you may need to really tackle your self-doubt-based procrastination?

_____

_____

_____

_____

_____

My plan to tackle self-doubt is: (Make a list of the action steps you plan to take to become proactive)

_____

_____

_____

_____

_____

Hopefully, taking a deeper dive into why you find yourself procrastinating will help you identify your triggers. If you find that you can't seem to break the habits even after working through these exercises, it may be useful to get some professional help. Therapists, coaches, or books can help you further explore your unique type of procrastination, and help you figure out how to overcome it for a more proactive lifestyle.

CHAPTER 11

Quick Tips to Stop Procrastinating Now

Sometimes you don't want to know why you are procrastinating, you just want to start getting things done.

Here is a quick list of tips to combat procrastination, boost productivity, and give yourself a boost of dopamine to feel better:

Goal Setting and Task Management:

1. **Set Clear Goals**
   - Define specific, achievable goals for tasks and projects. Having a clear target can provide motivation and direction.

2. **Break Tasks into Smaller Steps**
   - Divide larger tasks into smaller, more manageable parts. Completing these smaller steps can make the overall task feel less daunting.

3. **Prioritize Tasks**
   - Use techniques like the Eisenhower Matrix at www.productiveleaders.com/EisenhowerMatrix to prioritize tasks based on urgency and importance.
   - Tackle high-priority tasks first to reduce stress and increase productivity.

4. **Create a To-Do List**
   - Write down your tasks and deadlines. A to-do list helps you visualize your responsibilities and stay organized.

5. **Set Deadlines (Even Self-Imposed Ones)**
   - Establish deadlines for yourself, and treat them with the same level of commitment as external deadlines.

6. **Use Time Management Techniques**
   - Try techniques like the Pomodoro Technique www.productiveleaders.com/PomodoroTechnique, which involves focused work for a set period followed by

a short break.

7. **Minimize Distractions**
   - Identify common distractions in your work environment and take steps to minimize them. This might involve turning off notifications or finding a quieter workspace.

8. **Find Your Peak Productivity Time**
   - Determine when you're most productive during the day and schedule important tasks during those times.

9. **Limit Perfectionism**
   - Understand that perfectionism can lead to procrastination. Aim for "good enough" rather than perfection in your work.

10. **Eliminate Decision Fatigue**
    - Plan your day in advance, including what you'll wear and eat, to reduce decision-making fatigue and save mental energy for important tasks.

11. Use Technology Wisely

- Leverage productivity apps and tools like task managers, project management software, and digital calendars to stay organized and on track.

12. Set Realistic Goals

- Ensure that your daily your goals are specific enough to be crossed off a list. This clarity makes it easier to track progress.

Mindset and Motivation:

13. Practice Self-Care

- Be kind to yourself and recognize that everyone procrastinates at times. Avoid self-criticism and focus on improvement.
- Avoid negative conversations with yourself.

14. Use Visualization

- Visualize the benefits of completing a task, such as reduced stress, a sense of accomplishment, or achieving a personal or professional goal.

15. Stay Focused on the Outcome

- Remind yourself why the task is important and how it contributes to your long-term goals and success.

16. Seek Support and Guidance

- If procrastination is a persistent issue, consider seeking advice or coaching from a professional coach or counselor.

17. Use Positive Affirmations

- Develop a positive mindset by using affirmations to boost your confidence and motivation.

18. Practice the Two-Minute Rule

- If a task can be completed in two minutes or less, do it immediately instead of putting it off.

19. Learn to Say No

- Avoid overcommitting yourself. Politely decline requests or tasks that don't align with your priorities or capacity.

20. Delegate Tasks

- If possible, delegate tasks that others can handle, freeing up your time for higher-priority items.

21. Learn Time Management Techniques

- If it is important, schedule blocks of time on your calendar and adhere to that calendar.

Productive Work Environment:

22. Time Blocking

- Allocate specific blocks of time on your calendar for tasks and activities. Treat these time blocks as appointments and stick to them.

23. Task Batching

- Group similar tasks together and tackle them in one go. This reduces the mental effort required to switch between different types of work.

24. Create a Productive Environment

- Arrange your workspace for maximum efficiency. Keep it clean, organized, and free from distractions.

25. Visual Progress Tracking

- Create a visual representation of your progress, such as a checklist or a visual chart. Seeing your accomplishments can motivate you to keep going.

26. Accountability Apps

- Use apps or online platforms that track your productivity and provide statistics and reminders to stay focused.

27. Set Aside "Do Not Disturb" Periods

- Designate specific times during the day

when you won't entertain interruptions or notifications.

28. Limit Multitasking

- Focus on one task at a time to maintain quality and efficiency in your work.

29. Use the "Two-Minute Rule" for Digital Clutter

- Apply the two-minute rule to your digital life by quickly sorting and responding to emails, messages, or digital tasks.
- Play the "Unsubscribe Game." In your email search bar, search for the word "unsubscribe" and delete things that you are subscribed to that waste your time.

Self-Care and Well-Being:

30. Practice Mindfulness Meditation

- Incorporate mindfulness practices into your routine to reduce stress, improve focus, and increase self-awareness.
- Practice the deep breathing technique of 4-4-4. Breathe in for 4 seconds, hold for 4

seconds, and breathe out for 4 seconds to regain focus.

31. Practice Gratitude

- Reflect on the positive aspects of your work and life to boost your motivation and reduce negative thinking.

Remember that these tips can be adapted and combined based on your personal preferences and needs. Building a productive routine often involves a combination of these strategies to help you overcome procrastination and stay on track with your tasks and goals.

CONCLUSION

You can stop the procrastination cycle.

Procrastination is a habit. It's a type of resistance against things we don't want to do. Sometimes it's also resistance to things we *do* want to do.

Either way, procrastination isn't permanent.

You've got what it takes to stop procrastinating. To overcome procrastination, you need a little motivation and a solid plan to overcome your particular version of why you are stuck.

Hopefully, you've learned some important insights about procrastination, and now you have a solid plan for reducing procrastination in your life.

Remember to be kind to yourself as you start this journey. Many authorities claim it takes twenty-one days to create a new habit. If you've lived most of your life procrastinating, stopping certain behaviors and implementing others is going to take time. If you take three steps forward and one step back, you haven't failed. Get back on track and start again. Get help if you need it.

Here are a few tips that can make a positive difference to help you move forward:

Tip 1: *Use the buddy system*. Enlist a friend and make the commitment to become proactive together.

Tip 2: *Journal.* Journal your progress and your struggles, so you can see how far you have progressed over time.

Tip 3: *Educate and care for yourself.* There are many resources to help you drop the procrastination habit and become proactive. If you believe you need professional counseling, please get it.

Tip 4: *Don't delay.* Don't wait for the perfect time and situation to become proactive. Things will never be perfect. Timing will never be perfect. Start today!

Stay in Touch

I really enjoy connecting! I'd love to hear from you and celebrate what you found helpful!

Please consider signing up for my weekly resources on leadership, productivity, and business growth at www.ProductiveLeaders.com to stay current on information leaders consider valuable.

I am also on LinkedIn at:
www.LinkedIn.com/in/DrMaryKelly

In the meantime, be confident in yourself, and know that you can improve your results with a more proactive mindset.

I have more free resources on business growth, personal productivity, leadership development, and motivation at www.ProductiveLeaders.com/free.

I was honored and privileged to serve for twenty-five years on active duty in the Navy. Both of my brothers and my sister were military as well, so there is also a Veterans Resource link on that page, ranging from where to find veterans to hire to other links that veterans find helpful.

Let me know how what works for you! I am cheering for you!

Mary Kelly

Mary@ProductiveLeaders.com
www.ProductiveLeaders.com

ABOUT MARY KELLY

Mary is a graduate of the US Naval Academy. She served twenty-one years on active duty as an intelligence and logistics officer, mostly in Asia. She earned a PhD in economics, and she taught at the Naval Academy, the Air Force Academy, Hawaii Pacific University, and in the graduate school for Colorado State University.

She is the author of fifteen business and leadership books, including:

- The Five-Minute Leadership Guide
- 15 Ways to Grow Your Business in Every Economy
- Money Smart: How Not to Buy Cat Food When You Don't Have a Cat
- In Case of Emergency, Break Glass!
- Master Your World: 10 Dog-Inspired Leadership Lessons to Improve Productivity, Profits, and Communication
- Why Leaders Fail and the 7 Prescriptions for Success

- ❖ STOP PROCRASTINATING START ACHIEVING
- ❖ 5 Minutes Per Week and 52 Weeks to Building a Better Business
- ❖ Who Comes Next? Leadership Succession Planning Made Easy
- ❖ The AI Strategy Playbook

A member of the National Speakers Association, Mary was named to the Speaker's Hall of Fame in 2020. She is listed in the Top 50 World Sales Speakers, and as the 56th Most Influential Economist in the World. She is listed in the Top 50 Motivational Speakers List. She is consistently named as one of the Top Global Gurus in Organizational Culture.

Mary grew up in Texas, and she loves to spend time with dogs, her friends, and wine.

Made in the USA
Monee, IL
19 August 2024